ROUTINIZED

How the Organized Routine™
Routinizes the Work
That Elevates Success in Your
Business, Family, and Personal Life

Rick Carter

Published by
1KCapital, Inc.

Copyright 2015 by Rick Carter

All rights reserved.

ISBN: 978-0-9964664-2-4

Contributor

Dave Rasmussen

Editors

Kathleen Ellis

Maria Gagliano

Thank you:

Paul, Barbara, Larry, Mark, Stan, Nick, Rachel, Lisa, Kimberly, Tom, Andrea, Brydon, Joshua, Sam, Kim, Stan, Becky.

Contents

		Minutes to Read
Introduction		2
Chapter 1	Why	3
Chapter 2	How the Organized Routine Found Me	8
Chapter 3	Organize Plus Routine	4
Chapter 4	On, In, Out	4
Chapter 5	Four Types of Work	6
Chapter 6	What To Do with To-Do Lists	3
Chapter 7	How to Make an Organized Routine	5
Chapter 8	Two Dilemmas	6
Chapter 9	Organizing the Organization	5
Chapter 10	Your Two Greatest Assets	5
Chapter 11	Making Success Routine	4
Chapter 12	Try It Routinely	3
Summary		2
	Total Minutes to Read*	**60 minutes**

*at average adult reading speed of 280 words per minute

ROUTINIZED

Pronunciation and definition:

(ˈro͞ot – nīzed)

Two syllables. The middle "i" is silent.

To turn implicit, unrelated recurring tasks stored in the mind, triggered by previous action, and assumed completed, into an explicit Organized Routine™ of related tasks stored outside the mind, triggered by frequency, and openly accounted for.

Why write a book,

if not to change the world.

Introduction to *Routinized*

THIS BOOK IS FOR YOU

I've written this book with hope to make your day-to-day life even better. This is my vision: for you to elevate success and happiness in your daily life and in your life's endeavors.

My mission is to awaken, educate, and inspire you to see that *routine is the work of success and a source of happiness* in your journey toward achieving your big dreams, fulfilling your important responsibilities, and making your way successfully through each day. My strategy is to introduce you to the Organized Routine™ as the method for making routines work as you hoped they would by getting them out of your head and making them easier to stick with. My tactic for execution is a software application actually called "Tactick!™"

My primary purpose in writing this book is not to sell you Tactick; though, what is a good idea without a good way to put that idea into action? My purpose is to persuade you and show you how to routinize your business, family, and personal life. I promise you two results: more progress and more peace.

I've succeeded and failed, at little things, at big things. I've learned success is less a mysterious phenomenon for the lucky few, and more an available choice for the willing many. I've been grateful for my success. I've been frustrated with my failure, mainly because so much of it was unnecessary simply from not doing what I know I could have so easily done. We can't avoid failure completely nor can every endeavor be successful, but so much more success and happiness is within our reach.

THE 12 CHAPTERS

I start the book with the premise that success in life is based on routines. I also show how the Organized Routine makes life work better. Chapter 2 is the story of how the Organized Routine found me in the span of thirty-five years of success and failure in business. Chapter 3 explains how combining the boring nature of routines with the empowering nature of organization results in the new patent-pending process called the Organized Routine.

The already popular idea of working "on" something to get more "out" of something starts Chapter 4. It presents the Organized Routine as the method for acting on this idea. Chapter 5 puts routines in the context of the four types of work we do every day of our lives: routines, incidentals, projects, and problems. Chapter 6 talks about how traditional to-do lists don't capture the complexity of our lives, and Chapter 7 shows how to make an Organized Routine.

In chapter 8, I discuss the dilemma of choosing between two good things to do, and how the Organized Routine resolves that conflict. Chapter 9 explains how organizations work by implicit routines and how the Organized Routine makes organizations work better with explicit routines. Chapter 10 proposes the idea that people and process (the process being the Organized Routine) are equally important assets to an organization. Making success the rule versus the exception is the subject of Chapter 11. I close the book by proposing that routinizing life is how to get more out of life.

THE ORGANIZED ROUTINE CAN CHANGE THE WORLD

Individuals, families, and businesses have, do, and will continue to progress and succeed by routine work. We've done pretty well so far working from routines stored in our heads. We've made great advancements throughout human history and we have fairly successful individual lives without formalizing our routines, without the Organized Routine. The human race also did pretty well before industrialization and computerization. But look how much further we've advanced because of these.

Today we write our words in software not on paper, we calculate our numbers in software not on columnar pads, we manage our projects in software, we schedule our appointments in software, and we send our mail in software. It's time we organize our routines in software, not in our minds.

The world has talked about strategy for the last fifty years. Let's spend the next fifty years getting down to tactics, to action, to improving basic success in living and achieving. Let's routinize the world's work to make work easier and more available. Let's share with each other the routines that make our lives work. Let me show you how the Organize Routine is the structure to routinize the work that elevates your business, family, and personal success and happiness.

There is peace in
the rhythm of music,
the pattern of seasons,
the structure of time,
and the routine of work.

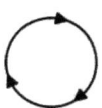

Chapter 1
Why

ROUTINIZE THE WORLD

Everyone wants to be happy, to do what they enjoy doing, to get joy out of life. Everyone wants meaningful relationships, to be needed, to have their needs met. Everyone wants to do what they feel is important, to make something of themselves, and to help others around them do the same. Everyone wants a successful, purposeful, fulfilling life.

Everything you want or need to accomplish in life takes work. It takes work to get a job done, and it takes work to avoid getting a job done. It takes work to make a relationship succeed, and it takes work to make a relationship fail. It takes work to do the right thing, and it takes work to do the wrong thing. It takes work to be happy, and it takes work to be sad. Simply put, work is how life works. Don't work at something you want and you won't see the results you want. Work at something you want and you'll see the results you want. Work routinely at something you want and you'll routinely see the results you want.

Life's outcomes are designed to be achieved by the routine work for each outcome. Grass is designed to be green by the routine work of watering. Muscles are designed to be strong by the routine work of training. The mind is designed to know by the routine work of learning.

Children are designed to grow by the routine work of nurturing. Marriages are designed to unify by the routine work of loving. Customers are designed to buy by the routine work of selling. The entire world, all of nature, and all that is in it, is designed to achieve its purpose by work done routinely.

But the routines of life are challenging. We may not have routines in place, or forget to do them. We may be bored by them or think they stifle creativity. We may think they interfere with life or even detract from life. We may not want to do them or even hate doing them. We delegate routines to others and wonder why they just don't get done. For most of us, routines are hard to make a routine part of our lives. And we have the outcomes to show for it.

That's why the Organized Routine is so important. A routine becomes an Organized Routine when it's taken out of your head and written down with its goal and with its related set of daily, weekly, monthly, and yearly tasks that make the routine's goal happen. Organizing routines makes them doable, bearable, and even motivating. The Organized Routine makes it simple to stick to routines, making them easier to do and even easier to delegate to others.

When we do the routine work of life with Organized Routines, life works better. We have more time to live life, more brain space to create new things, more energy to do what we really want to do, and best of all, perhaps, more peace of mind, and more progress. One day we'll look back and wonder why we ever wasted so much time, effort, energy, and hope doing the routine work of life and goals from our heads and not through Organized Routines.

Routinizing is not a new idea. Routinizing with the Organized Routine is. Many books and articles have been written promoting routinizing to businesses and individuals as a way to increase success and reduce the cost of effort. How to actually structure and execute routines has been missing. The Organized Routine is how.

So spend the next sixty minutes reading this book, then spend the rest of your life experiencing the power of Organized Routines, and join us in our mission to routinize the world's work to better humankind, one business, one family, one person at a time – starting with you.

WHAT I MEAN BY . . .

Routine:

1) An activity, task, or a set of work done again and again and again to complete a job, achieve a result, or accomplish a goal;
2) a set of work stored in a person's memory and triggered by a previous action;
3) necessary work often considered monotonous, mindless, or menial.

Organized Routine:™

1) A structure for a person's or a group's recurring tasks organized in a unified, clear, and purposeful set of work;
2) a method to get routines out of one's head and into action;
3) a process for delegating work and holding others accountable.

Tactick:™

1) A software application made for storing and executing recurring tasks as Organized Routines;
2) process- or task- management software for managing the tactical work of completing a job or achieving a goal;
3) an alternative to paper, a spreadsheet, a calendar, or other software for storing and executing recurring tasks.

Routinize:

1) To turn implicit, unrelated recurring tasks stored in the mind, triggered by previous action, and assumed completed, into an explicit Organized Routine of related tasks stored outside the mind, triggered by frequency, and openly accounted for.

Improve your emotional health:

set and keep routines.

↻

Chapter 2
How the Organized Routine Found Me

A Quick Thirty-Five Years

I grew up in an organized home, with an organized family life. My father also had an organized work and community life that I admired. Everything seemed perfect. Everything that needed to happen seemed to always happen, and the outcomes were pretty good.

When I started my own home, family, work, and community life, I couldn't figure out how to achieve the same level of organization. Things just didn't work that same way. I thought my parents must have had "that something" and I didn't, and I was concerned I couldn't achieve the outcomes I wanted. But I was determined to discover what "that something" was—and that was the start of my thirty-five-year journey.

I began to look around to see how things worked, specifically how the organizations of marriage, family, business, and community worked. When I got my first real job, managing a medical clinic in 1980, I didn't ask, "What is this business's core purpose?" That seemed obvious: deliver medical services to patients. But that was the doctor's job. What I really wanted to know was, what was my job? I asked, "How do we make sure the right support work gets done to achieve our core purpose?" That was my job as manager. I had learned that businesses not only need to know how to do things the right way, they also need to have a way to make sure the right things get done.

So, I met with others in similar roles. When I asked them how they organized the support work that sustained the business's main work I was simply shown to-do lists. When I asked about routines or patterns for this work, they commented, "Oh, well sure, of course I do that." "Do you have that written down somewhere so I can learn from it?" I asked. No one did. I asked them how they remembered so many things, how they could organize and execute so many functions and processes just from their head. "I just do," was their response.

At first, I figured they were like my parents. They just had something that I didn't. So over the next couple of years I wrote down every task I did each day. However small or big, however meaningless or important, I meticulously wrote it down. For each thing-to-do, task, job, or goal I was given or decided to do, I wrote down the work necessary to accomplish it.

I then sat down and sifted through my dozens of pages of lists and categorized the tasks. Work I did once and was quick to do I called "incidentals." Work I did once, but took a long time to do I called "projects." Work that popped up without warning, that demanded immediate attention and consumed far too much time (and that was usually caused by not doing the right thing in the first place) I called "problems." Work that I did over and over again I called "routines."

The largest category of work was "routines." These recurring tasks kept the many parts of the company consistently working—

everything from marketing to operations to finance. These were the ordinary maintenance tasks that needed to be done to keep the lights on, people happy, and revenue flowing. These routines were also how I made steady progress toward achieving goals.

I organized the recurring tasks into four categories I called "drivers": product, market, money, and manage. I called them drivers because these four categories drove business success. Have a working product or service, have a market that wants it, have money to keep activity flowing, have people to do the work, and you have a business.

I documented the process of managing by routine. I organized the recurring tasks into jobs, gave the jobs goals, and then organized the jobs under the drivers. I needed reliable triggers that would act as reminders to get the recurring tasks started, so I applied daily, weekly, monthly, or yearly frequencies to every task in each routine. I now had a system for how the business worked, and a process to keep it working.

As I organized and worked according to these routine tasks, I found that I not only had fewer unexpected incidentals, I had fewer problems, and the problems that did arise were easier to deal with and didn't grow into crises. I didn't get so absorbed in incidentals and problems that I would forget to routinely conduct staff interviews, or routinely look at monthly reports. But the best part was, I wasn't using my brain to keep track of the routines, and I wasn't trusting that somehow they would just happen. I had more mental bandwidth and time available to think about business improvement and work on projects. I felt more confident. And, I felt like I was starting to achieve the level of organization and accomplishment I had grown up with.

By 1985, I was consulting with a lot of medical clinics. I used my "routinization" system at clients' offices and they loved the organization and structure. I now had a system that helped me personally run a business and that helped me help others run their businesses.

I soon left my consulting work to own and operate a chain of medical clinics. Things didn't work out too well. I fell into the same trap as many small business owners: I focused too much on my projects, didn't maintain my operating routines, and ended up losing everything.

A bit deflated but still determined, in 1990 I went back to consulting for a short while and continued refining my system of drivers and routines. When one of my clients asked me to build a business from scratch, I took the job. This was my first chance to build a business from its first dollar, its first task. I implemented my system and ran it using a spreadsheet and a calendaring software program. I also started assigning routine tasks to other people. Being able to tell people specifically what was expected of them daily, weekly, monthly, and yearly, and how those recurring tasks fit into jobs with goals, made it easier to delegate work, hold people accountable, and keep them motivated by showing how their efforts were connected to the entire business. The business grew five-fold in the next two years and hit industry benchmarks. I now knew my system could be implemented in a startup setting and help grow a new business better and faster.

There's simply no way to efficiently keep track of hundreds of tasks with different frequencies across many people with a spreadsheet and calendaring system, let alone on paper. So, in 1995, I took six months off work to build a software program for organizing, storing, and executing routines. I hired a programmer and started giving demos. I needed a name for the software. I called it "The Everest System of Organized Routines." The premise was that running a small business is like climbing Mount Everest. Whenever there is a lofty goal, achieving that goal is more about following structure and routine than relying on luck and sheer strength. I showed The Everest System demo software to owners, managers, and parents. Everyone said, "I would love to use that," so I continued to advance the demo software to useable software.

Before I could complete the software, I ran out of money and had to go back to work. So I once again went back to consulting and over the next 10 years built a successful practice inside a mid-sized consulting firm. In 2005, I decided to leave the firm I was in and start my own consulting firm. By 2010, I had grown my firm from $0 to $6 million and 40 people. While doing the consulting work *in* the business, I also made sure to do the management work *on* the business. How did I do both successfully? My Everest System of Organized Routines. It was the first thing I implemented and I used it to effectively organize, run, and grow the business.

In 2012, I sold my firm. A business associate encouraged me to focus my efforts on bringing The Everest System to the world of small business. Then one day, Dave Rasmussen, a business colleague and long-time friend, showed up at my house. Dave was gainfully employed, but wanted to do something more fulfilling. I told him about the Everest System and how Organized Routines worked.

We talked about jobs, tasks, structure, and accountability. I talked about how small businesses benefit from this system. Dave had a background of personal success. He suggested that the system of Organized Routines is applicable not only for small businesses, but to any organization where working *on* the organization enables the organization to achieve its purpose more easily. In other words, it's applicable to families, businesses, teams, schools, community organizations, and even individuals (who also need a way of making sure they hold themselves accountable to routinely get the right things done). How committed was Dave to his suggestion? He quit his well-paying job and went to work on the Everest System and Organized Routines full time.

With the help of branding experts and software programmers, we changed the name of the software to "Tactick" and launched the first version in April 2015.

At the beginning of my career I asked the question, "How do we make sure the right work gets done to achieve our purpose?" Thirty-five years later, I have my answer in a book: Routinized! I ask the same question going forward, "How do we make sure the right work consistently gets done in life?" I have my answer in a software tool: Tactick.

I want to share both with you in hopes they will help you as much as they help me.

My Vision for the Organized Routine

My vision for Organized Routines is to increase success and reduce failure for people in their businesses, their families, their teams and organizations, in every part of their lives—through the science of Organized Routines. I want to see people spend more time *in* doing what they enjoy doing and get more *out* of life by consistently working *on* the ordinary routines of life and using routines to achieve more of their life's goals. As a society we can avoid more of the high failure rate of small businesses, reduce the increasing collapse of marriages and families, and de-escalate the incidence of personal unhappiness if we simply turn life's ordinary but necessary work into simple and accountable routines.

Like climbing Mount Everest, building your business, family, marriage, or personal life involves a considerable amount of hope and risk. But success isn't about big, bold decisions or the occasional exertion of massive effort; it's about the constant, rhythmic pattern of sticking to routines, of keeping commitments you make to yourself or others to routinely do what needs to be done.

When scaling any of the mountains of life, success is influenced by many factors, many in our control. A common factor in all achievement, and one we can control, is doing the ordinary routine tasks that lead to success. Yes, we do need courage, creativity, and intuition in life. But, if we go at it with these alone and don't maintain the routine work of life, we almost always achieve only a part of our goals. Yes, discipline, attentiveness, and persistence are ingredients for continual success. But, when those traits aren't in us in abundance, we often give up and decide we are among the have-nots.

Success doesn't take super-human effort, just ordinary, consistent effort. I know the word "consistent" is a big part of the problem. We all make commitments to ourselves or others to do things routinely and then we don't stick to them. This is not because the work itself is that hard, but because we forget or get distracted or don't remember why we're doing it in the first place. In fact, I see too many people work too hard to achieve their goals, then accomplish too little, and be frustrated along the way. This is not because we aren't willing to work hard, but because our work process often isn't effective.

Most of our time is spent attempting to reorganize episodic, disconnected effort, or figuring out what to do versus doing it. Our minds are often busier than our bodies. Worry seems like actual work. Organizing itself sometimes becomes the goal, and days are full of starting and stopping, getting on and off track. We rely on heroic, high-energy, inefficient episodes of hard labor instead of on simple, quiet, low-cost effort.

The thing is, this ordinary routine work may not make us feel extraordinary, but it gets results. Routine has a bad rap for being mundane and stifling. Even the word sounds tiring and lifeless. But routine is transformed when organized with detail, accountability, and purpose. Routine then takes on a whole new life. And when routines are organized on paper or automated in some type of software like Tactick, accountability and consistency become the rule instead of the exception. You decide once, and do it routinely.

Organized Routines transform the way we work. Organized Routines can do for knowledge work what the Industrial Revolution did for manual work. Mass production gave us more goods, produced for more people, by more people, at a lower cost. The Organized Routine lets more people do more efficient work to produce more output with less effort. That can mean better GDPs, GPAs, and ROIs. Organized Routines replace wasteful unproductivity and frustrated ambition with effective work and fulfilled goals. We can have more jobs, more productivity, and more economic expansion as work is better organized and available to more people through a better process: the Organized Routine.

The Organized Routine may not change the kind of person you are, but it will change how you work and what you achieve. Whether you're an organized or a disorganized person, whether you like or dislike routine, or whether you think structure helps or hurts creativity, Organized Routines help you have better outcomes and more joy in the process.

My goal in writing "Routinized" the book and creating "Tactick" the software is to give you both an inspiring idea and a practical tool you can use to do more with your life and get more from your life whoever you are, whatever you believe, wherever you're starting from. All you have to do is start with one recurring task you want to make sure you do every day, week, month, or year.

Structure, order, and routine
are inside us.
They can drive us crazy
or drive us forward.

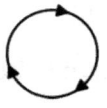

Chapter 3
Organize Plus Routine

TALK ABOUT BORING

The word "routine" has a bad reputation. We ignore routines or do the ones we remember and feel like doing, not wanting to waste precious time and energy on them. We think we're above them or that they're in our way.

Consider some of the dictionary definitions of "routine":

- A procedure, practice, pattern, drill, or regimen
- Regular performance of an established procedure
- Of commonplace or repetitious character
- Ordinary course of events, having no special quality
- Duties done regularly or at specified intervals

And consider the synonyms for "routine":

habitual, unvarying, unimaginative, dull, uninteresting, commonplace, placid, rote, grind, tedium, monotony, banality, groove, boredom, chore, doldrums, dullness, sameness, lifeless, drab, dreary, mundane, boring, predictable, tiresome, run-of-the-mill, humdrum, mind-numbing, uninspired, accustomed, chronic, conventional, familiar, general, methodical, normal, periodic, plain, standard, typical, unremarkable, usual

Sounds pretty bad! Sounds unworthy of our best efforts. Sounds like our lives sometimes. Sounds like what we live to avoid. In fact, many of us believe that routines can lead to one of these conditions:

- Rut: a settled and monotonous routine that is hard to escape
- Rat Race: an exhaustive routine with no time for relaxation
- Robotic: mechanical, stiff, unemotional

TURNING THE TABLES ON ROUTINE

Surprisingly, if we look at the definition of "organize" we find an entirely different and more enjoyable perspective:

- To form into a coherent unit or functioning whole
- To integrate separate elements into a single structure
- To arrange elements into a whole of interdependent parts
- To form into coordinated parts for united action
- To arrange into a desired pattern or structure
- To arrange systematically for harmonious action

And the synonyms for "organize":

arrange, adapt, adjust, be responsible for, catalogue, classify, codify, combine, compose, constitute, construct, coordinate, correlate, create, dispose, establish, fashion, fit, form, formulate, get together, group, harmonize, line up, look after, methodize, mold, put in order, put together, regulate, run, take care of

Doesn't this sound a lot better? The definition of organize feels refreshing, relieving, hopeful. Maybe this is why so many of us may not organize our routines, but we certainly routinely organize. We love organizing so we keep doing it, over and over and over, again and again and again, but without the type of results we seek. Often, when we don't get the results we want we simply keep trying some new method. Organizing itself becomes a way of feeling like we're making progress. But by itself, organizing doesn't get things done.

PUTTING IT ALL TOGETHER

Now combine the definitions for "organize" and "routine":

- To form into a coherent unit or functioning whole then do as a sequence of actions to be followed regularly

- To arrange into a desired pattern or structure then do as duties to be completed regularly or at specified intervals

- To arrange systematically for harmonious or united action then do as a prescribed, detailed course of action to be followed regularly

ORGANIZE + ROUTINE = THE ORGANIZED ROUTINE (PATENT PENDING)

Organized Routines are about the structure and the content: replicable, repeatable content that is clear, unified, and purposeful. But the structure of organize + routine is what gives the Organized Routine its power. A routine task by itself is hard to stick with so it becomes powerless. This is because we try to store most routines in our minds. Routines stored in the mind fade away from conscious memory, become disconnected from the thoughtful purpose of why we're doing them, and compete with thoughts of doing something else. Over time the mind perceives routine tasks as more and more difficult compared to the actual act of just doing them, especially if we hate doing the tasks we know we should do. The unfit person hates going to the gym and thinks about why they hate it, then they don't go. The fit person also hates going to the gym, but they don't think about it and they just go.

However important the routine is or however committed you are to it, in the moment when the planned routine work should be done, you face two challenges: remembering to do the routine and deciding, again, to do it. Again, the mind is not the place to store routines. The Organized Routine is where to store routines. The Organized Routine takes routine work out of the mind. It organizes and stores the planned routine, remembers when and who and reminds why. When it's time to do the routine work, the Organized Routine lets the mind focus on doing the work and not on remembering and re-deciding whether or why.

Think of the Organized Routine as a recipe, a "work recipe." A food recipe is a set of steps for preparing a particular dish, including a list of the ingredients required and how to combine them. A work recipe is like a food recipe. It's a set of steps for completing a particular job or achieving a goal, including a list of tasks required and how to combine them.

The Organized Routine gives hope. If you want to make sure you routinely do something, routine + mind is a sure way of not sticking with it. But routine + organize in an Organized Routine gives you the power to stick with the routines that make your daily life more fulfilling and your life's endeavors more achievable.

What Organized Routines Look Like

① Driver/Area
② Job/Goal
   ③ Recurring Task   ④ Assignment   ⑤ Frequency

HOUSE
  Lawn-Enjoy Being in the Yard

Recurring Task	Assignment	Frequency
Mow the Lawn	Tony	Weekly
Fertilize the Lawn	Tony	Quarterly
Aerate the Lawn	Tony	Yearly

FAMILY
  Marriage-Stay in Love

Recurring Task	Assignment	Frequency
Say I Love You	Nan, Bill	Daily
Arrange a Date	Nan	Weekly
Arrange Anniversary	Bill	Yearly

MARKETING
  Sales-Hit Revenue Targets

Recurring Task	Assignment	Frequency
Send 5 Emails	Murphy	Daily
Update the CRM	Pat, Tom	Weekly
Complete Sales Report	Tom	Monthly

MIND
  Read-Keep Mind Sharp

Recurring Task	Assignment	Frequency
Read Morning Book	Hannah	Daily
Read Travel Book	Hannah	Weekly
Attend Reading Club	Hannah	Monthly
Read at Big Sisters	Hannah	Monthly

SPORTS
  Baseball-Play Together

Recurring Task	Assignment	Frequency
Play Catch	Dad, Fran	Daily
Confirm Play Site	Dad	Weekly
Clean Uniforms	Mom	Weekly
Schedule Players Mtg	Dad	Monthly

It takes commitment
to pursue a big goal.
It takes even more commitment
to do the simple,
step-by-step, routine work
to get there.

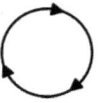

Chapter 4
On, In, Out

WORK ON YOUR GAME

People who have to repeatedly create or manufacture exacting products understand the value of explicit routines. If you go to a great culinary school you'll find students learning very precise procedures for their profession. I'm not only talking about recipes. I'm talking about how to run a kitchen. How to manage every part of a restaurant has been painstakingly analyzed and written down, and students are tested and graded on how well they know and execute these procedures. A theatrical play is built on routines that are carefully laid out and written down and understood by every member of the cast and crew. The script, of course, but also where the actors are to be at every moment, where each piece of scenery is to be placed at what time, and which lights are to be used for each scene.

These are just a few of the many routines that no professional chef or director would expect a successful production to happen without. These routines are necessary to work *on* the core purpose of what the chef and director really want. The chef doesn't want a kitchen, he wants a great dish. The director doesn't want a stage, he wants a great play. But unless they work *on* the ordinary routines, they won't continue to create great work *in* the business.

The apparent paradox is that the constraints of routines to work *on* one's core purpose are a pivotal part of what allows artistic expression to flourish. The truth is, structure and process provide the foundation for freedom and authenticity in endeavors within any organization, whether it be a culinary school, a play, a small business, a family, a marriage—even the organization of self.

When you do the *on* part of your life, you can spend more time being *in* your life and get more *out* of your life. For the chef, this might mean having more time to create innovative dishes and experiment with new techniques. The chef is not only doing more of what he loves to do, but he's getting closer to achieving his big goal in life to become one of the most respected and well-known chefs. Getting more *out* of life is achieving the things you most want—happiness, time, money, health, spirituality, knowledge, good relationships, and so on. These things are our big goals, the dreams we have for our lives. But each of us has unique ways of getting there depending on who we are and what we like to do.

Being *in* your life is doing what's core to your unique self, what you really want to do, what you love to do, your passion. On the other hand, working *on* your life is doing the ordinary, but necessary work of life to get there. These tasks often seem like they hold us back. Quite the opposite! If you don't work *on* your life, you tend not to do as well as you want with the *in* or the *out* parts of life.

Here are more examples:

- A tennis player is being *in* his game when he's playing an opponent. He's working *on* his game when he's practicing, working out, or watching videos of his performance.

- A hair stylist is being *in* her business when she's doing hair. She's working *on* her business when she's ordering supplies, training a new stylist, or sending out email reminders to regular customers.

- A doctor in medical practice is being *in* her business when she's visiting with a patient or doing a procedure. She's working *on* her business when she's conducting staff meetings, looking over the books, or reading medical journals.

- Parents are being *in* their family when they're reading to their children, playing games, or having dinner together. They're working *on* the family when they're shopping, doing laundry, or cooking dinner.

Most of us don't choose to be parents so we can do laundry or go shopping. But if we don't do these everyday tasks, having time to be with our children is more difficult and more stressful. And we don't get the joy out of our relationships. Doctors don't choose the medical profession so they can do payroll or manage staff. But if these tasks aren't done in an organized way by someone, it's more difficult to maintain a smooth-running office that supports excellent patient care. And they don't get the professional satisfaction they seek out of their careers.

Being *in* the passions of life is easy. These are the interesting, fun, exciting, motivating, fulfilling activities, and usually the actions that bring the most financial and emotional rewards. They're the things we want to do first. They drive our lives and make us feel alive. Working *on* life isn't as interesting, and yet it is so important.

How to Work On

Working *on* the ordinary tasks of life is not so easy. They're mundane, boring, and usually don't come to us instinctively. They're not what we're trained to do and seem to always get in the way. We wish someone else could do them for us, but when we delegate, we struggle with the burden of making sure others are accountable to get done what needs to be done.

The idea of working *on* your business, your profession, or your life is not a new idea. Using Organized Routines to work *on* your life is a new idea. Organized Routines help people work more efficiently *on* their life and get better results *out* of their life.

Organized Routines tackle the *on* part. They allow you to stay focused on the *in* part while not neglecting or being annoyed by the *on* part. They do this by converting the *on* work into complete sets of reliable, recurring tasks that happen at specific frequencies. For example, to get the benefits from air conditioning in your home, the work *on* your air conditioning needs to be done: replace filters quarterly, service pumps annually, clean ducts twice a year, set temperature monthly. The Organized Routine takes these tasks out of your head, off of your to-do list, and puts them into one list, one time. Now you can forget about them until you're prompted.

Not having explicit routines for working *on* your life often results in lousy timing. "If only I changed the filter when I was supposed to, the air conditioner wouldn't have conked out during the hottest day of the year." "If only my staff were regularly trained they could have handled the dozens of customer calls that came in after we launched the new marketing campaign." "If only I had kept up with my monthly reports, we would have enjoyed more insights from our planning meeting." So many times crises are simply the result of not working *on* the ordinary routines of life.

Organized Routines are for working *on* life. They let you spend more time being *in* your life to get more *out* of your life. This is because life works by routines, and routines work better when they're organized.

There is joy in routine,
not only in the outcome,
but in the very process
of doing it.

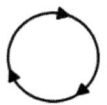

Chapter 5
Four Types of Work

ROUTINES, INCIDENTALS, PROJECTS, AND PROBLEMS

To-do lists, appointment calendars, and other organizing methods only go so far in helping us manage recurring tasks. It's not that to-do lists don't have their place. It's just that we expect too much from them. But when we start using Organized Routines, these other tools can function the way they're supposed to.

To understand how these methods work together to help organize our lives, it's important to revisit the concept of "work." At the core of the Organized Routines system is the fundamental principle that all of life takes work—the negative, the positive, the fun, the mundane. There are no shortcuts. But most of us think of work only as negative, something we have to do and often try to avoid. The Organized Routine changes the negative related to work. The thought of work in our heads is far more painful than the actual work when we do it. The Organized Routine gets work out of our head and into action. Putting routine work into some type of structure makes the work we may not want to do, but need to do, simpler and easier to do routinely. Now we have more time to do the work we really want to do. That's revolutionary!

The work we do in our individual, family, and business lives typically falls into four categories: *routines*, *incidentals*, *projects*, and *problems*.

Routines. By now you should be getting the picture. Routines are sets of recurring tasks that we do again and again. They make up most of the ordinary work of life and are how we consistently work toward achieving goals. Doing the "payroll" routine, for example, is made up of a number of tasks that are done every two weeks, or every month. The "taking care of the yard" routine is made up of many tasks that are supposed to be done on a recurring basis. For most of us, the "retire wealthy" routine is made up of routinely putting money in the bank.

If you gather up all your to-do lists over the past several weeks or months, you will notice that most of the items are actually repeated or recur at some frequency. No wonder we find ourselves making the same to-do lists over and over again! Herein lies a fundamental problem with to-do lists. Some routines may happen twice a year—like replacing smoke detector batteries. Do you remember to write that down on your list twice a year? Or do you wait until the buzzer goes off in the middle of the night, only to realize that you also haven't routinely refreshed your supply of nine-volt batteries?

If your job is payables, you have a few options: you can choose to write down the tasks, over and over, week after week; or, you can dispense with the list and rely on yourself and everyone else involved with payables to remember all the tasks all the time; or, you can write the tasks down once in an Organized Routine. The second approach, the "I'll just remember everything in my head and hope everyone else does, too" method is quite common and is one of the main causes of problems, and gaps in process when someone leaves.

Most of life's work is recurring. At the same time, much of life's work is simple. But we make it harder than it needs to be. It's pretty much impossible for the human mind to keep track of hundreds of planned and unconnected tasks that fall on specific days. Converting routine work into Organized Routines makes life's work significantly easier to do.

When you start your day, first look at your routines. Then look at your incidentals, then your projects, and finally the problems. Working in this order will prevent problems, will get incidentals out of the way and get others on their way, and will free you to focus on projects and other important activities that you want to do. If incidentals take up your day every day, examine them. Many of them are probably recurring tasks.

This book is about routines. My main point is that if you get more organized with your routines and apply them to your jobs and goals, you'll not only have fewer incidentals and problems, but you'll have more time for projects and simply being more present *in* your life.

Incidentals. Incidentals are one-time tasks that take a short time to complete, are easy to do and, most importantly, aren't repeated. Incidentals are little things that can get us on our way to other, more important tasks. Many times they are tasks we promised others we would do; they are like little task debts. Getting our incidentals done helps others get on their way, too.

Incidentals can develop into problems if we don't do them in a timely manner. As an example, your co-worker, Bob, emails you and requests that you send him a file you talked about at the regular morning meeting. This is something Bob needs to get on his way, and you're part of that happening. If you don't do your small part, Bob can't do his. Incidentals are often a way to serve others and prevent problems that could take a lot more of your time later, as well as create conflicts in relationships.

The best place for incidental tasks to live is on standard to-do lists. Unfortunately, most of us try to shove any and all tasks that come our way onto these typical to-do lists, which is a key reason why to-do lists are so long, unwieldy, and overwhelming.

So how can you tell if a task is an incidental? When an item on your to-do list comes up, ask yourself, "Is this a one-time task or is it really a task or part of a job or goal I need to do daily, weekly, monthly, or yearly?" If it is, put it in an Organized Routine. If it isn't, then it's an incidental and belongs on your to-do list.

Projects. We've talked about incidentals and routines. Projects are big, one-time jobs. They're often the type of work we really want to get to because they propel our lives forward. Projects typically require us to gear up and gear down, and entail thrusts of focused efforts and large chunks of time over a sustained period. For the owner of a small business, finding time for important projects, like researching and implementing a new marketing campaign, can often mean the difference between success and failure.

Though projects are not routines, routinely working on projects results in more progress than relying on "when I have time" or ignoring everything else. If you're used to "building Rome in a day," you will find building Rome daily works better.

Problems. Problems are issues that stop us in our tracks and take precedence over other priorities. Though most of us have fewer problems than we have incidentals and routine tasks, problems are what we often face day to day. A flat tire, a sick child, a client with a crisis. Problems, and what we do about them, usually don't end up on our to-do list because we don't plan for them, and we usually have to take care of them immediately.

Problems come in two forms: naturally-occurring and self-made. Life has built in, *naturally-occurring problems*: Jason fell at school and needs to get immediate medical care. The office manager contracted a virus and has been home from work for three days. A recession has caused the housing market to tank, affecting the number of construction jobs for our business. These kinds of problems are out of our control. But how well we handle them is often determined by what *is* in our control—the routine work of life, the incidentals, and the projects.

Many of the problems that plague us and wreak havoc in our lives are s*elf-made problems.* These problems usually happen when we don't maintain this routine work of life. We keep forgetting to weed the garden until the job takes most of Saturday instead of half an hour. The office manager has all her routines in her head, so when she's out for three days things fall apart. But these kinds of problems are in our control. Let's change the story: the office manager creates Organized Routines for every key part of her job, making it easy for someone else to jump in for three days. Or, a dad creates an Organized Routine for gardening and is reminded when it's time to weed. Keeping the garden routinely weeded and watered allows the family to get away for a weekend at the beach instead of spending it doing clean up. And creating the routine also makes it easier for him to delegate the weeding task to his kids, so they can learn to work in a structured, orderly way.

LIVING ROUTINELY

So if living routinely helps prevent many self-made problems, why is it so difficult to do and why don't more people do it? Problems are noisy, flashy, and unrelenting. Problems demand attention now. Routine work, on the other hand, is quiet and simple. It's easy to ignore. Routines let you choose to do them, or not. Problems don't.

And sometimes we just "don't feel like it." Routines are set in advance of when we do them. They never show up at a convenient time. There is usually something else we feel like doing. But, we always do something. It's just whether it's something you decided you want in your life, or whether it's something you just feel like doing in the moment.

Some of us are hooked on the rush and self-adulation of solving big problems. We might even let things break down, just so we can save the day.

At some point we have to just stop and switch gears. Instead of being so controlled by self-made problems and impulsive feelings, we can to choose to live routinely, which makes it easier to get the routine tasks done that actually make life work. At some point we have to stop reacting to life, and start creating the life we want. As we do, most of our self-made problems will disappear, and our impulsive feelings will be replaced by confidence, peace of mind, and sustained progress.

Even tasks that should be born of our souls work better when routinized. Telling our spouses we love them or playing with our children or visiting our parents or checking in with key customers should just happen because we care. Right? But, how would it make you feel to see your spouse write down that they want to make sure they tell you "I love" every day? Or your child sees you are so committed to them that you purposefully organize around routinely being with them? Routinizing life means getting the "should do" tasks out of your head and heart and turning them into the consistent action of "actually do."

Living routinely is an all-in proposition. It's hard to live organized and disorganized at the same time. You either follow routines or ignore them. Using Organized Routines doesn't mean you'll never procrastinate or fall behind. And doing routines for routine's sake doesn't work for most people. That's why purpose and goals are so important to the structure of an Organized Routine. Being accountable by checking off routine tasks is satisfying. Taking care of recurring tasks without a lot of stress starts bearing fruit. Now there's more time for projects, more time for being *in* life, more time for being with people and getting more *out* of life. Living routinely is living supremely!

Our biggest goals
deserve the best of our
structured, organized,
routine effort.
How else do we achieve them?

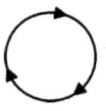

Chapter 6
What to Do with To-Do Lists

THREE PROBLEMS WITH TO-DO LISTS

We all know that organizing work makes doing the work easier, and most of us have some method of organization. We often use some type of outline or to-do list to remind and motivate us to do what we need to do, or help us keep track of what other people are supposed to do. Some people use deadlines as organizers: as the deadline looms and the stress mounts, the work starts getting done. None of these methods are very effective.

The most popular method for getting organized is the traditional to-do list of random items thought up in the moment and then prioritized. Regardless of where they live—on paper or a whiteboard, online or in an app—traditional to-do lists share at least three problems.

The first problem with to-do lists is *we expect too much from them*. Whether you use an organizer, an app, or the back of receipts, your lists are most likely repetitive, with the same to-dos getting shuffled from day to day and week to week. It's unrealistic to expect isolated, random to-dos on a list to capture the complexity of our lives, let alone simplify it. We continually get organized, only to get organized again. We never get organized to stay organized. We routinely fall behind and feel the frustration that comes with consistently failing to accomplish what we need to do or want to do.

Part of what's so frustrating is that we know many of these tasks just aren't that difficult or time-consuming. The thought of the work is so much harder than the work of the work. How hard is it to pull a few weeds in the garden? To make a few calls to customers? To replace the air filter? To take a few minutes to connect with our spouse or play with our children? But it's easy to procrastinate or avoid these relatively simple tasks when most of us spend so much time putting out fires and managing chaos that seem to crop up everywhere, in spite of our to-do lists.

The second problem with to-do lists is that *many tasks never make it to the list at all*. They seem too small, too simple, too ordinary, or even too routine to actually write down. Yes, sometimes we'll create a list of tasks after we've completed them just so we can get the little endorphin rush that comes from checking off a bunch of tasks, but we rarely write down every little thing we have to do beforehand. Instead, we use an enormous amount of mental energy to remember dozens of details and rely on memory to tell us what we've accomplished and what we still have left to do.

The third problem with to-do lists is *orphan tasks.* Orphan tasks are actually recurring tasks often disconnected from sibling recurring tasks that are all part of a family of recurring tasks that work together to complete a job or achieve a goal. These jobs and goals and their associated tasks are what the Organized Routine brings together. When tasks get disconnected from the overall job and its purpose—why we're doing the job in the first place—we're less motivated to get them done.

Let's look at a typical approach to organizing the "take care of the garden" job. This job is made up of a number of tasks. You might put "weed the garden" on a separate to-do list every week. "Buy plants" might get put on another family member's list every year. "Water the garden" probably won't make it on anyone's list until the garden looks terrible and it becomes a clean-up project that you don't have time to take care of. "Check fertilizer and buy more if needed" might not make it to the list until you go to plant your flowers in springtime and discover that there's not enough left from last year. The result? Gardening plans foiled, time wasted, motivation gone, and you haven't taken care of the garden—the job you wanted to accomplish through all these scattered to-dos. Your goal of sitting *in* your delightful garden sipping a cool drink fades because the ordinary, everyday tasks of working *on* your garden have fallen through the cracks.

The solution? Clear off orphan tasks from your to-do lists. Stop re-writing them and instead put these tasks into Organized Routines! As described earlier, an Organized Routine is a set of recurring tasks related to the same specific job or goal. With Organized Routines, each task is given a specific frequency and is assigned to a specific person. This gives your recurring tasks a permanent home and makes them "sticky." Because all the tasks are listed out beforehand, you don't have to spend your mental energy trying to remember them. Because Organized Routines are built around the job each recurring task helps fulfill, all tasks that are part of the same job are in the same place.

Over the last hundred or so years we've evolved into a reasonably successful, to-do-list people. But the to-do list hasn't evolved. It solved the problem of getting our work, plans, hopes, and dreams out of our head and onto paper, making us more effective. Now it's time to take the routine work off of our to-do lists and into Organized Routines, resulting in even more effective action, but without as much effort. Simply put, Organized Routines cost less and deliver more than to-do lists.

Routine is not the enemy,
but is the foundation
of creativity.
Paint daily.
Dance weekly.
Write monthly.
Explore yearly.

↻

Chapter 7
How to Make an Organized Routine

FIVE STEPS

Creating an Organized Routine is easy. You can use a pencil and paper, a spreadsheet, or a calendar. You will end up with many tasks organized in sets of routines scheduled across several frequencies probably assigned to various people. Using some type of automated software application, like Tactick, will make it easier to store and execute many tasks and routines.

Chapter 5 described the four types of work: routines, incidentals, projects, and problems. The distinctions are important because you'll need to look at the jobs you're responsible for and the goals you want to achieve and then organize them. Incidentals are one-time tasks that belong on to-do lists. Projects are usually done whenever we have time, and we might use a specific project management tool for large, complex jobs. Problems are usually dealt with immediately.

The rest of the work we do is made up of the ordinary, recurring tasks we do over and over, daily, weekly, monthly, or yearly. These are the tasks we tend to store in our heads and hope that we'll remember to do them at the right times, or repeatedly write down on lists. These are the tasks you turn into Organized Routines.

Here's a list that breaks common tasks into either incidentals or recurring tasks:

    Task: Pick up dry cleaning
    As a Recurring Task: Weekly pick up drying cleaning Fridays

    Task: Put on snow tires
    As a Recurring Task: Annually put on snow tires 1st week Dec.

    Task: Email Tom's address to Jim
    Incidental: not part of a routine

    Task: Buy a new remote for the TV
    Incidental: not part of a routine

    Task: Finish financial statement
    As a Recurring Task: Monthly finish financial stmts. 10th

    Task: Run 2 miles
    As a Recurring Task: Daily run 2 miles

    Task: Talk to Marina about messy room
    Incidental: convert to a recurring task for Marina

    Task: Prepare for meeting on 3/24
    As a Recurring Task: Monthly prepare for staff mtg. 2nd Wed.
    Incidental: not part of a routine if not recurring

Now that you have a better understanding of what kinds of tasks go into Organized Routines, you're ready to take a look at your own life. Examine a few weeks of your to-do lists. Or write down the tasks you did during the past week. You're looking for recurring tasks that go together. For example, you probably spent time doing things in the kitchen. A friend of mine told me that if she had a refrigerator routine she would have been reminded to vacuum the coil and grill. She would have seen that the ice cube maker hose was starting to come loose, and probably could have prevented a messy and costly repair when the hose broke and flooded the kitchen.

When you're ready to start making your own Organized Routines, follow these five steps:

1. **Create a name for the job or goal.** To keep an Organized Routine simple to do and easy to understand, use a noun to describe it.

    >Dog
    >Social Media Marketing
    >Workout

2. **Put your jobs or goals into categories.** I call them drivers because they drive success in each area of life.

    >Business: Product, Market, Money, Manage
    >Family: Marriage, Children, Culture, Home
    >Personal: Mind, Body, Spirit, Heart

3. **List the recurring tasks that belong to the job.** Use an action verb to describe each task, making it clear and easy for anyone to understand what needs to be done.

    >Walk the dog / buy dog food
    >Post content to sites / review stats
    >Mow the lawn / buy fertilizer

4. **Choose a frequency for each recurring task.** This is the Organized Routine's secret ingredient. Think of what you do daily, weekly, monthly or yearly to accomplish the routine. Some recurring tasks are done quarterly or every six months. You might not remember each task when you first create an Organized Routine, especially a task that's only done once a year.

> Twice daily walk the dog
> Monthly buy dog food
>
> Daily post content to sites
> Weekly review social media analytics
>
> Weekly mow the lawn
> Yearly buy fertilizer
>
> Every other week go on a date
> Yearly buy anniversary present
>
> Quarterly submit taxes
> Yearly complete tax return

5. **Assign the recurring tasks.** All the tasks are yours, of course, if you are organizing yourself. But, if you're organizing your family, business, community group, start-up, or team, then assigning is the fun part. After you make an Organized Routine with all its recurring tasks it's easy to see what can be delegated to others, and it's easier to hold them accountable.

I have friends who share a car. Here's an example of their Car Routine:

CAR

- Weekly buy gas   Eva
- Weekly log miles   Pete
- Monthly clean car   Pete
- Monthly check oil   Eva
- Yearly rotate tires   Eva
- Yearly change car oil   Pete
- Yearly re-register   Eva

Here's an example of a pre-built Organized Routine from Tactick's library:

Social Media Marketing
Build our online presence
Tactick
BIZ Market

D W M Y	TASKS
1 DAILY	Produce content for posts
2 DAILY	Post content to sites
3 WEEKLY	Review social media analytics
4 WEEKLY	Email social media report
5 WEEKLY	Monitor competitors' posts
6 MONTHLY	Plan social media contests
7 MONTHLY	Review social media campaigns
8 MONTHLY	Use infographics in posts
9 YEARLY	Update social media strategy

SIX TIPS FOR MAKING SUCCESSFUL ORGANIZED ROUTINES

1. **Start slow.** It takes some time (maybe ten minutes) and mental effort to create an Organized Routine. But once created, it takes care of itself. Don't sit down and think about dozens all at once. Start with one or two and build them over time.

2. **Make an Organized-Routine Routine.** Make one of your routines your "Organized Routine" routine. Daily check off tasks, daily enter new tasks, weekly check on progress, monthly revise routines and tasks, etc.

3. **Capture the Moment.** It's much easier to make a routine and identify its recurring tasks when you are in the moment. It's hard to just sit down and out-of-the-blue think up the daily, weekly, monthly and yearly tasks to do some type of routine you haven't thought of or done in a while. Capture and write them down when they happen.

4. **Verb the Noun.** Write routines as nouns and recurring tasks starting with a verb then a noun. I call it "verb the noun." So the routine is "dog," and one recurring task is "walk the dog." Or the routine is "sales," and one recurring task is "complete the report," or "call the customer." Once you do a few you will get the hang of it. A common way of describing work helps everyone easily understand what you mean and creates a common way of communicating.

5. **"What" not "How."** Recurring tasks are the "what" not the "how." The problem with most accomplishment is not that we don't know how to do something, it's that we don't do it routinely. Organized Routines assume you know how to do something; they simply help you do it routinely.

6. **Progress not Perfection.** Even though your life becomes more organized with Organized Routines, you still won't accomplish every recurring task at each frequency. But with Organized Routines, you're more likely to do a recurring task more often than you did before. This means more progress toward your goals and more fulfillment of your responsibilities. And, remember: acknowledging accountability to routines is as important as actually getting them done.

Organized Routines are a new way to engage life, and to find life more engaging. It's worth the initial time and effort to set up. You will increase your peace of mind. You will have more time. You will have less worry. You will get more things done. You will make more progress. You will have less conflict with others. Others will understand and do what you need them to do. You will keep more of the commitments you make to yourself and to others. You will live life much more proactively and less reactively. You will act more and be less acted on. You will be more in control and be less controlled. You will live by choice, not by instinct. It does take time, it's a different way to approach each day, and it's worth it.

The work toward a seemingly
unimaginable outcome,
unreachable ideal,
or unattainable goal
can be broken down
into daily, weekly, monthly,
or yearly acts of
imaginable, reachable, attainable,
routine effort.

Chapter 8
Two Dilemmas

DICHOTOMY AND PROPENSITY

I grew up in a part of town where small businesses kept opening and closing in a set of buildings I passed by frequently. I noticed the closed signs on businesses so often I finally asked my father about them. "Someone had a dream and then they lost it," he told me. "A closed sign on a business means 'dream over.'"

I have both failed and succeeded in business. Failing is, in one word, terrible. Upon reflection I realized that much of the failure I experienced didn't need to happen. I would have significantly increased the likelihood of staying in business by consistently doing the common, ordinary, simple routines of working *on* the business. Instead, I did what came naturally, versus doing both what came naturally and what needed to be done. Businesses have needs independent of whether we want to meet them or are capable of meeting them, or not.

DILEMMA ONE: DICHOTOMY

(dichotomy: a division of things into two contradictory parts)

All small business owners face the same challenge: how to work effectively *on* the business while at the same time working to succeed *in* the business. By the way, the same is true for the boss at home who faces the challenge of how to effectively do the support work *on* home life while at the same time doing the main work of being *in* the lives of those at home.

Let me explain. You come to work at your small business and you face two types of work. The first type is being *in* your business, doing the main work you love to do, the reason you started your business: selling the flowers, making the cabinet, fixing the motor, singing the song, answering the customer's questions, painting the house, finishing the tax return, pulling the tooth, writing the code, baking the pie, taking the picture. This is what you wish you could do all the time, and you could if you didn't have to face the second type of work, the support work *on* your business: meeting payroll, setting prices, hiring staff, improving product, promoting, paying bills, raising capital, analyzing trends, stocking shelves, cleaning equipment, determining raises, conducting meetings, collecting receivables, filling orders, buying supplies, depositing checks, training staff, renting space, organizing, planning, designing processes.

This is a dichotomy—the choice we set up in our heads between what we want to do and what we need to do to keep the business running smoothly. We say to ourselves, "I can either sell my flowers or order supplies—I can't do both." "I can either be at the front counter making sales or be in the back office doing inventory—I can't be in two places." "I can work on quality or deal with finances—I have to choose one over the other." A parent managing a small enterprise called 'home' says, "I can have time with my kids or have a clean house—I can't have both."

This second type of work, the administrative, support, or maintenance work, is part of every small business. It comprises the ordinary, recurring tasks that always seem to get in the way of the more exciting, more fulfilling first type of work, the type of work you love to do, the reason you started your business in the first place. Not only that, you might not be very good at the support type of work. You might wish you could trust others, or wish you had enough money to hire others to work *on* the business so you could focus more *in* the business. Even if you do hire someone, you still need a method to organize the *on* work, keep them on the same page, and hold them accountable.

You know being *in* your business is essential. Without you doing the main work you're good at there are no customers, no cash flow, and no business. But simply being *in* your business isn't enough. To grow, to survive, to thrive, to fulfill your dreams and your hopes and your goals, you also have to work *on* your business. Being *in* your business is the heartbeat, but working *on* your business keeps the lights on. Taking the *on* work out of your head and putting it into Organized Routines resolves the dichotomy.

DILEMMA TWO: PROPENSITY

(propensity: an inclination or natural tendency)

The second dilemma business owners face is business propensity, the inclination or tendency to focus on their strengths, versus taking care of the four key business drivers equally: product, market, money, and manage.

For example, some owners have a natural inclination to focus almost exclusively on finances, dismissing marketing efforts as not being worth the investment. Other owners focus on product quality while missing management's critical deadlines. Most business owners understand that their business needs a good product, a market that knows about and wants the product, sufficient money to keep the business alive, and effective management to keep all drivers working together. But few owners have inclinations to drive all four areas equally.

This propensity, or leaning toward one driver over another, creates a number of serious problems. A business too heavy in product tends to have low sales. A business too heavy in marketing tends to overspend. A business too heavy in finance tends to take too few risks. A business too heavy in management tends to over control.

What many small business owners tend to forget is that all four business drivers are important. Large businesses that can afford multiple managers solve the business propensity dilemma by hiring people with specific inclinations and strengths for each driver. Small business owners, without large budgets, can resolve their business propensity dilemma by organizing and executing the Organized Routines that keep all four drivers working efficiently. The owner leaning toward finance, for example, probably doesn't need to be prompted to routinely check on the bank balance, but does need to be reminded to check on social media trends. The owner leaning toward product probably doesn't need to be prompted to improve a key feature, but does need to be reminded to communicate with staff on company performance.

So as a boss, owner, or manager how do you overcome the dilemma of being *in* your business or working *on* your business? How do you balance your propensity toward one business driver over another? You organize the ordinary routines of working *on* your business so you stay focused being *in* your business.

SOME ORGANIZED-ROUTINE BUSINESS ADVICE

When talking with struggling small-business owners about Organized Routines, they often say, "You're telling me that doing basic, ordinary routines will bring in more customers, add more revenue right now, or increase my profit?" My answer is, "Absolutely not. The basic maintenance of routines doesn't directly bring in business—you do, by being with customers, following up on orders, and developing new solutions. But your business is in trouble, which means either you never get around to doing the things that create results, or once you get results you can't maintain them because you have no infrastructure, no way to keep things routinely working."

Even the highest level of activity that produces results is best done by routine. For example, I routinely connect with past customers—and I routinely get new business this way. If you ask a business owner who lacks revenue or customers when they last reconnected with former customers, they will probably tell you an anecdote or two. On the other hand, a business owner who can tell you how many calls were made each quarter of the last six quarters is usually too busy to tell anecdotes because they're swamped with customers.

I once managed a business for a start-up with a single owner and one employee. One year later the business had had grown three-fold in revenue. How did this happen? Among other things, I implemented Organized Routines on day one. Yes, even with one employee and one owner we had routine financial reviews, routine staff meetings, routine connections with suppliers, routine reports of customer utilization. Even though you could count the number of customers, transactions, and reports on one hand in the early days, the routines laid a foundation for high-impact yet routine work, such as checking in with customers quarterly. Three years later after the business had grown eight-fold, I moved on, but the routines remained in operation. That was over twenty years ago. The business is still running today.

Functioning with Organized Routines gets into the heart of a business. It helps create culture, a tangible personality for the business. People know what to expect. Once you have staff saying, "We always…" "Every week we…" "Every month we…" then you know you're building functional tradition and culture.

Remember the question capital investors always ask about a business when considering its value? "Are there key processes in place such that, if the owner or key manager left, the business would still at least operate?" Organized Routines provide a way to develop operational assets that don't rely on the owner and that are a value-add to a potential investor or buyer.

A note to non-profit service organizations: if your work is the support of people and not profits, use Organized Routines to organize and execute the "administrative" work of people, and then you'll be free to "minister" to the needs of people. Ignoring the mundane, routine tasks of administration in favor of only serving your people puts you in debt to the organization that your people rely on. In all organizations, committing to work *on* earns you the freedom to enjoy being *in*.

People are willing to work,
as long as they don't have to
think about it.

Chapter 9
Organizing the Organization

ORGANIZATIONAL ROUTINES VS ORGANIZED ROUTINES

A small business, a team, a family, a marriage, any type of group can be an organization. An organization exists when 1) two or more people are involved in a common cause, 2) they have expectations of each other to actually get something done to advance their cause, and 3) they are willing to be accountable. Passing by a tennis court one day, I overhead one player say to the other "from now on let's play tennis every Saturday." The other player said, "Okay. I'll schedule the court each week. You drive every week." An organization was formed.

Usually someone in an organization is recognized or is chosen as the one in charge: the head, the leader, the boss, or the person all others are accountable to. Even when two people are equal in an organization someone usually says, "Well, I'll be in charge of this and you be in charge of that." Eventually most organizations end up with some type of formal authority and accountability structure, with someone giving direction and expecting others to do something, and someone or a set of people receiving direction or assignments and doing what someone else wants done. In larger organizations there are layers of these superior and subordinate structures up and down a hierarchy.

So how do things get done in organizations, especially the ordinary work that keeps an organization running? All organizations work by executing routines. Sports teams execute routine plays. Cooks execute routine recipes. Dancers execute routine steps. Actors execute routine scripts. Musicians execute routine scores. Businesses execute routine jobs. Families execute routine chores. The sequences of work unique to how each organization functions make up its *organizational routines*.

Organizational routines become the culture, the traditions, the "way things are done here," and usually they're not written down. They're implicit, not explicit. Too often, they simply evolve without too much conscious thought. Organizational routines are informal, even though they support formal work. Examining organizational routines more closely will help illustrate how they work.

THE FORMATION OF ORGANIZATIONAL ROUTINES

A small business owner finally has the cash flow to hire an employee and they hold their first meeting; or a group of individuals comes together to form a new company, club, or association; or a newlywed couple sits down to talk about running their new household. At the end of the first meeting they say something like, "Let's meet every week, and can you arrange the meeting place, and I will make sure we have an agenda?" An organizational routine is born.

Here's another example: the CEO tells the CFO, "This is a good way to look at our cash flow. Could you send this report to me at the end of every month?" This routine (sending the report) is not only a recurring event, it's also a sequence of recurring tasks that must be completed by a number of people in a specific sequence to ensure that the report will be ready at the end of the month. On the fifth business day of the month, the books are closed by the bookkeeper. This is the trigger for the accountant to put the data into summary form, which she then sends to the administrative assistant. This is the trigger for the administrative assistant to formulate the final report and deliver it to the CFO. This triggers the CFO to review the report, make final adjustments, and send it to the CEO.

Throughout this sequence, numerous cues or triggers prompt each person when it's time for his or her part in the routine. In fact, triggers are essential in understanding how organizational routines work.

The following scenarios highlight the crucial role triggers play across organizations.

- A baseball centerfielder knows that when a runner is on first and a ball is hit, that's the trigger for him to throw the ball to the second baseman. If he doesn't know or complete his routine, the team doesn't advance its cause.
- An actor knows that when another actor says a particular word, that's the trigger for her to enter stage left.
- A child knows (or hopefully remembers the trigger) that on Wednesdays he has to put his dirty clothes in the laundry room. That triggers the child's mom or dad to do the laundry and put the clean

clothes on his bed, which is then his trigger to put his clean clothes away.
- A staff member uploads her timesheet at the end of the month, triggering the finance clerk to summarize the billings, which triggers the billing manager to submit the invoices to clients so the company has revenue next month.

In every organization, hundreds of these trigger-driven organizational routines form over time. Stand and watch a business or family operate for a week and you'll find that the majority of activities are organizational routines stored in the organization's "memory" or "hard drive;" meaning, in the collective minds of the people in the organization. The crucial thing to remember is that whether the organization is a business or a family or a team, its performance and results are based on the successful completion of its organizational routines.

THE FORMAL ORGANIZED ROUTINE

Organized Routines are formalized organizational routines: Organized Routines are explicit, not implicit. They're written down instead of kept in people's heads. They're intentionally created and triggered by specific frequencies instead of previous actions. And the biggest difference is they're checked off to ensure accountability.

Sequences in organizational routines can break down because they're forgotten, unclear, not triggered, or misunderstood. For example, if the accountant gets sick and doesn't complete her task, the administrative assistant may not realize this until it's too late and the report for the CEO doesn't get completed by the deadline. Or it's Thursday and you remember it's also garbage day, but the kids haven't emptied their trash into the main bin. Or you remember you wanted to post on social media for your business every Friday, but you don't know if the copywriter finished the weekly draft.

Or take the story of a manager who has just been hired. When most employees start a new position, they're given some kind of job description often spoken and not written. Typically, this description includes a general listing of jobs and responsibilities. For our new manager this might include production reports. But when that report is to be generated at the new job, versus the former job, and how that task is related to other tasks, is usually left to the new employee to figure out. Which means the new employee must quickly search the company's implicit hard drive to uncover what organizational routines have been developed to produce the reports. This means a lot of time spent asking different people questions about how things are done, hearing different interpretations, considerable time wasted, and, most likely, expectations unfulfilled. Mistakes happen not because the manager doesn't know "how" to do, but because he or she doesn't know the sequence of "what" to do in the context of the new organization. This is called a learning curve, and too often it's much slower and costlier than necessary.

Generally, businesses and organizations allow their hard drive, their organizational routines, to reside in people's heads. This puts the ordinary, but necessary, work of running things constantly in jeopardy. There are simply too many variables that can go wrong, lowering the percentage of times expectations are met. Organized Routines, on the other hand, transform organizational routines into clear, explicit, replicable sequences where reliability and accountability are built-in, increasing the number of times expectations are met.

The study of organizational routines has been the focus of organizational-behavior academics for over fifty years. The Organized Routine is a breakthrough, practical application of the organizational routine that can now be used to advance existing organizations beyond today's levels of performance, and give new organizations an increased likelihood of succeeding sooner and succeeding longer.

Routines channel creativity,
just as schedules channel time,
banks channel rivers,
and laws channel freedom.

Chapter 10
Your Two Greatest Assets

PEOPLE AND PROCESS

According to accepted wisdom, this is the era of the "knowledge worker." Knowledge workers, people, carry their ideas, experiences, and insights with them, making the people the most important assets in any organization. Here's a different perspective: Organized Routines, together with people, are the two most important assets in an organization.

If an organization doesn't have Organized Routines, then people do become the most important asset because they carry the hard drive of the organization in their heads. They know both what to do and the sequences for doing it. We rely on them to carry out the vital routines that keep the organization running. When we see people doing good work we think it's because they know "how" to do something. Mostly, however, it's the organizational routines they do that make them so important. They know "what" to do. This insight is one of the most overlooked opportunities for an organization to increase success.

When we hire new employees, we're hiring the hard drives they bring with them. We give new hires some training and general job descriptions, but mostly we're hoping they'll bring hard drives that will fit in to our organization. But this approach is costly and inefficient. In all my years building and running businesses, I've found that less than half of what a person brings to a new role is applicable.

Once we realize that most of the work in an organization is a collection of organizational routines, mostly mundane, ordinary work, the value of creating Organized Routines is immediately evident. Organized Routines can transform the way we work because they make the implicit become explicit: they take implicit organizational routines out of people's heads and turn them into explicit Organized Routines that people can see and adapt to.

The beauty of Organized Routines is that you only have to describe each routine one time. Once you've finished, you'll have the "what to do" for every key part of running your organization. And you'll have a platform for evaluating and making jobs work better. Now you can continuously improve the Organized Routine. Organizational routines that are kept in people's heads or that people bring with them are aspects of an organization that deteriorate. Organized Routines are assets that stay in the organization. Organized Routines become an organizational asset that reduces dependency on just the natural talent of people. We create jobs that can be done by more people because the jobs are now more explicit.

We are attracted to people we want to hire because we're impressed by their talent, their ideas, their ability (or potential) to innovate. Taste and talent is important when it comes to the higher level work in the knowledge economy. You want the writer, designer, engineer, with just the right philosophy or aesthetic that you're looking for. But let's face it: how many of us have dealt with a brilliant person who doesn't consistently deliver? How often have we said, "I'd rather have someone who does an 'OK' job and does it all the time, than someone who can 'rock the universe,' but you never know when?" We can increase the likelihood of actually reaping the benefits of great talent with Organized Routines. So we need to find the right people and give them our Organized Routines, and then we can have more confidence that the people hired will be accountable to consistently deliver the thing that drew us to them in the first place—the high-level and unique thinking that separates an individual from a sea of other potential candidates in the knowledge economy.

REDEFINING MICROMANAGING

Using Organized Routines is micromanaging in the best sense. It's what I call "giving clarification just one more layer down." Management by objectives is a good idea. Executing by routines makes it work. Groups perform better when everyone knows what they have to do, when accountability is built-in. Organized Routines give people the structure they need to be successful. People talk about wanting freedom and opportunity to innovate in their job. But over thirty-five years I can tell you that I've heard many more employees say, "They didn't tell me what they expected."

Groups can become functional faster and more functional overall if routines are set in place. Purposefully establishing them in the form of Organized Routines can accelerate performance. This happens because groups need a process to rely on before results actually occur.

Groups rely on routines, rhythms, structure. Organized Routines give groups a framework to build trust and provide reliability before patterns of accomplishment have been achieved.

Here's an example: A marketing manager I worked with, I'll call him Tim, was dedicated and hard working. He was resourceful and creative. What more could you want? Results. Tim didn't feel he was getting the results he wanted and the business owner felt the same. The owner, I'll call him Bill, started doubting Tim's abilities and thought he was wasting time—a typical response many owners and bosses feel when they don't see results and they can't see the work in process. Trust and hope were eroding on both sides.

I had Tim and Bill sit down together and set up Organized Routines for marketing. They organized daily social media routines, weekly social media impact reporting, weekly website maintenance, monthly production of new content, weekly sales meetings, and monthly job reviews. Two months after Tim started consistently doing these routines, three things happened: 1) results improved, 2) Tim felt more confident and his satisfaction grew from the work, and 3) Bill stopped complaining and gave Tim recognition for both his effort and results. Trust was rebuilt and a reliable structure was now in place to give hope of continuing positive results.

But could it really have been that easy to change results? After all, if it was that easy, everyone could do it. That's right! That's exactly what I'm saying. Results are more available to more people more easily with Organized Routines. Tim was already working with social media, making new content, and maintaining the website. Each time he was *in* doing it, he did it the right way. The problem was he didn't routinely choose to do the right thing, to work *on* it routinely. He didn't have the consistent focus necessary to make something work routinely. It wasn't the quality of Tim's work, the "how," it was the consistent quantity, the "what." And Bill's part was that he had not managed "one more level of clarification down." He hadn't given Tim the structure he needed to be successful, because he didn't want to micromanage. But the result was no accountability on either side.

Using Organized Routines is how a manager can actually manage without being controlling. It's *micro-management without micro-control*. A manager using Organize Routines empowers the group without overpowering the individuals. Organized Routines takes the guesswork out of good work: "Here's where we've decided to go, how we plan to get there, who's doing what routinely, when it's to be done, and confirmation that it's done." Now both the group and the individual can get to doing.

Wouldn't it be great if the employee could read the boss's mind? And if the boss's feelings that something is or isn't done were accurate? Working with others isn't easy. But it can be made easier with simple clarification, structure, accountability, and acknowledgement. Organized Routines make working with others easier, and they make it more enjoyable for others to work with us!

When it comes to sticking
to routines,
the mind is a terrible thing
to trust.

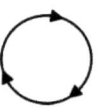

Chapter 11
Making Success Routine

EVERY DAY

How often do you need to do a task in an Organized Routine? Daily? Weekly? Monthly? Yearly? The answer depends on the nature of the job or goal. Changing the furnace filter is a yearly routine in some places, monthly in others. Changing the filter daily is unnecessary and doesn't improve the performance of the furnace. Exercising could be daily or weekly, depending on your goal. Choosing the right frequency is important. The key to all routines, however, is consistency. Here's a story that illustrates the value of consistency in a daily Organized Routine.

In many businesses the revenue cycle, the process of billing and collecting from customers, is critical to success. But each step of the revenue cycle must be completed every day. Not *some* steps completed every day, not *most* steps completed *some* days, but *each* step, *every* day. Maintaining this daily process is the key challenge and main reason why revenue cycles so commonly underperform, resulting in either decreased revenue or increased cost of collecting, or both.

Special projects (usually a euphemistic name for solving problems) often draw attention away from the revenue cycle routine. This is a typical scenario: As the revenue starts underperforming, panic ensues, and a special project is triggered in an effort to get caught up or solve the revenue crisis. The revenue cycle routine stops, as time and resources get directed to the special project, results continue to drop, and getting caught up usually doesn't fully happen.

I had a client with a revenue cycle underperforming by several million dollars. When I asked about daily processes, I got the typical answer: "Yes, we do this particular revenue cycle routine daily." Yet when I examined the data, I could see that the process wasn't done every day. When I showed this data to the client his response was, "Oh, you mean 'every' day, like each and every day? Well, in that case, no.

I helped my client organize around consistent routines and one year later, not only did they experience a multi-million dollar increase in revenue, but they established processes that sustained this improvement each year going forward. Was this success due to new staff? No. Was it new processes? No. Was it special skill available only to a few people? No. This success was due to a simple recommitment to the structure of the daily revenue cycle routine and the allocation of sufficient staff to get the work done routinely—and the measurements to prove it.

This solution to maintenance of ordinary routines is available to every business, to every organization, to every team. Here's a simple example that illustrates Organized Routines at home: My friend's wife tells him the laundry room has an odd smell. My friend checks out the dryer. The filter is full and smells of mildew. He replaces it and the smell vanishes. His wife asks, "How often are you supposed to replace that?"

"I'm not sure," he answered, "but I'll find out and set up a routine so I won't forget, instead of waiting for a smelly laundry room."

SUCCESS IS A CHOICE

Organized Routines are not habits. Organized Routines are proactive. Habits are reactive. Organized Routines are a choice. Habits aren't a choice, they're instinctive. Success isn't about building more and more and more habits inside of us that are unconsciously done so we don't have to choose what to do. We have the choice to let unconscious habits run our lives. We also have the choice to run our lives by conscious routines. And, we have the choice to let nothing at all run our lives.

Habits can lead to outcomes we don't want, like the habit of not completing production reports so the plant manager can allocate resources; like the habit of taking all the cash out of the business so the payables manager can't pay bills and suppliers end up not delivering; like the habit of doing what we want to do, not what is right to do. The worst habit of all is the habit of ignoring routine.

Whether success happens or not is influenced by what we do control and choose to do, and by what we don't control and choose not to do. Occasionally, success is thwarted because of events that happen in spite of our best intentions and actions. But generally, success is controllable; it's a choice. Our work is to find the controllable actions that lead to the kind of life we want and then consciously choose to do them routinely, not to rely on the development of unconscious habits.

Every now and then, someone has success because of something they did once or twice; this is called luck. Success is sometimes chance, but mostly it happens because what we maintain leads to a desired outcome. An athlete usually wins because of repeated preparation, training and practice, not because of one or two spurts of activity. A garden is beautiful because of many factors, but primarily influenced by repeated, regular watering, weeding, and feeding, not because of a flurry of activity on a single weekend. A student becomes a scholar because of regular study. A retiree is usually secure because of regular restraint in spending and regular saving of money. A devotee usually gets in tune not because of a single life-changing event, but because of regular, repeated acts of devotion. A business owner is successful not because of one deal, but because of repeatedly serving the customer and regularly taking care of the business.

By simplifying the process of creating repeatable, regular actions, and by structuring these actions so they're tied to our goals and dreams, Organized Routines help us see the mundane for what it is—the necessary work that will help us be more engaged *in* our lives and achieve more success.

If you're bored with life,
do routines.
If you're bored doing routines,
they're working.

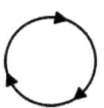

Chapter 12
Try It Routinely

ONE MONTH

Organized Routines can be a hard sell. Organized Routines are based on structure and detail, both of which are difficult for many people to give in to without some type of simple method they can rely on. Even when people hear that the majority of what makes life work and goals achieved is ordinary, recurring tasks, they're still a hard sell! What makes the difference is when someone tries Organized Routines and has the first "aha!" moment; the first realization that it's not too difficult to get those recurring tasks out of the way; the first exhilarating sense of freedom from worry; a new feeling of being more in control; and getting work out of their head and into action.

I have a friend who has three children and a very busy life. For her, just trying to keep things from descending into chaos is challenging. I suggested she try Organized Routines for a month. I figured she was ready because she had spent years trying to make to-do lists work, from creating piles of sticky notes to using smartphones.

It took my friend a few days to create some routines with her most important goals focused on relationships. She wanted to spend more quality time with her family and less time feeling overwhelmed with cleaning, cooking, and generally managing the household. After the month was over, I asked her to report in on how she was doing with Organized Routines. This is what she told me (after she reminded me again that she is not naturally a very organized person):

> "At first it felt strange having all the tasks for the household programmed. But I just made the decision to try it. Now I love having all my routines organized in one place. It took a couple weeks, but now it feels natural to check my task screen the night before so I'm ready for the next day. I'm finding that jobs that have always seemed so difficult are actually pretty simple to get done now that they're part of a routine. And it's such an adrenaline rush to check things off and see how much I've accomplished! I've started feeling much more empowered. I always thought I had to make a choice between being a good mom and having a well-run household. Now I know I can do both. One thing that surprised me was how positively my kids have responded to the structure. They like the routines, especially since I now have more time to spend with them. I'm beginning to understand that anything is possible if I create the routines to support what I want to do. Of course I'm not perfect, but more often than not I'm doing my routines regularly. I can see the freedom in that and it's very exciting!"

My goal in writing this book has been to explain in clear, practical terms how more businesses, more families, and more individuals can climb their Mount Everest as well as maintain fulfilling day-to-day lives through routinely taking care of the ordinary work to get there. I believe the phrase "by the sweat of your brow" need not be brute force, or overworking, or painful work, but good work, effective work, and fulfilling work. I want to re-enthrone the value, the very necessity of work. I embrace structure, order, accountability, consistency, and routine as foundational to happiness, productivity, and fulfillment.

As the Organized Routine revolutionizes the way we all work and live, the possibilities are limited only by our ability to create and stick to the routines that will make them a reality. I see more freedom for more people to produce even more extraordinary and fulfilling outcomes for themselves and others. I see more time for more people to be *in* their lives and get more *out* of their lives. All by routinizing life, by getting routines out of their heads and into organized action.

Try Organized Routines for a month, routinely, and let me know what happens!

rickcarter@tactick.com

Routinize the work in your
business, family, and personal life
with the Organized Routine™
in Tactick™
and you will elevate
the success and happiness
in your life.

A Chapter Summary of *Routinized*

My purpose is to persuade you and show you how to routinize your business, family, and personal life. I promise you two results: more progress and more peace.

1. Life's outcomes are designed to be achieved by the routine work for each outcome.
2. Success isn't about big, bold decisions or the occasional exertion of massive effort; it's about the constant, rhythmic pattern of sticking to routines, of keeping commitments you make to yourself or others to routinely do what needs to be done.
3. Routines stored in the mind fade away from conscious memory, become disconnected from the thoughtful purpose of why we're doing them, and compete with thoughts of doing something else. Over time the mind perceives routine tasks as more and more difficult compared to the actual act of just doing them.
4. Organized Routines are for working *on* life. They let you spend more time being *in* your life to get more *out* of your life.
5. At some point we have to just stop and switch gears. Instead of being controlled by problems and crises, we have to choose to routinize life to make it easier and simpler to actually get the routine tasks done that make life work.

6. A problem with to-do lists is orphan tasks. Orphan tasks are actually recurring tasks often disconnected from sibling recurring tasks that are all part of a family of recurring tasks that work together to complete a job or achieve a goal.
7. Start slow. It takes some time and mental effort to create an Organized Routine. But once created, it takes care of itself. Don't sit down and think about dozens all at once. Start with one or two and build them over time.
8. How do you overcome the dilemma of being *in* your business or working *on* your business? How do you balance your propensity toward one business driver over another? You organize the ordinary routines of working *on* your business so you stay focused being *in* your business.
9. Organized Routines are formalized organizational routines: Organized Routines are explicit, not implicit, and they're written down instead of kept in people's heads. They're intentionally created and triggered by specific frequencies instead of previous actions.
10. Organized Routines, together with people, are the two most important assets in an organization.
11. Generally, success is controllable; it's a choice. Our work is to find the controllable actions that lead to the kind of life we want and then consciously choose to do them routinely, not to rely on the development of unconscious habits.
12. As the Organized Routine revolutionizes the way we all work and live, the possibilities are limited only by our ability to create and stick to the routines that will make them a reality.

GET ROUTINIZED!

www.ingramcontent.com/pod-product-compliance
Lightning Source LLC
Chambersburg PA
CBHW071156090426
42736CB00012B/2347